THE LITTLE BOOK OF

MASSIVE COCK-UPS

THE LITTLE BOOK OF MASSIVE COCK-UPS

An Hachette UK Company
www.hachette.co.uk

Summersdale Publishers Ltd
Part of Octopus Publishing Group Limited
Carmelite House
50 Victoria Embankment
London
EC4Y 0DZ
UK

www.summersdale.com

Printed and bound in the Czech Republic

ISBN: 978-1-78685-782-8

Substantial discounts on bulk quantities of Summersdale books are available to corporations, professional associations and other organizations. For details, contact general enquiries: telephone: +44 (0) 1243 771107 or email: enquiries@summersdale.com.

Disclaimer
All facts are correct to the best of the author's knowledge at the time of going to press.

THE LITTLE BOOK OF

MASSIVE COCK-UPS

A BRIEF HISTORY OF EPIC FAILS

JAMES PROUD

summersdale

INTRODUCTION

Everybody makes mistakes, and nobody's perfect. It's no big deal – until it is. Sometimes, cock-ups are so momentous that they stand the test of time and are even worthy of recording in the history books. There is no precise equivalent in English for the German word *Schadenfreude* – deriving entertainment from the misfortune of others – but if there were, it would definitely apply to this catalogue of catastrophes.

Some of the enormous errors in this book were down to bad judgement; some were the result of laziness or plain bad luck; many are classic cases of hubris and vanity. Whether it's misplacing nuclear weapons, passing up on billion-dollar business deals, losing an empire or offending half the world's population on social media, all of these slip-ups have had far-reaching consequences, some of which are still being seen today.

These top-notch failures are unbelievable, ironic, tragic and often amusing, but they all share an oddly attractive characteristic: they allow us to indulge in the strange pleasure of reliving mistakes we didn't make ourselves.

HOWLER AT THE MOON

We've all seen the grainy footage of Neil Armstrong making his "small step" onto the surface of the moon in 1969, yet apparently, we are lucky to have seen it at all. The famous moonwalk was shot using a format that provided high-quality images, but which could not be transmitted directly to television sets. By the time the signal had been beamed from the moon and converted for broadcast via a radio telescope in Australia, the final image quality was much degraded.

In 2006, NASA decided to use modern technology to enhance the original images sent from the moon, so that the historic moment could be seen in the best possible quality. But when they started looking for the rolls of film that they assumed were in their archives, there was nothing to be found. Three years later, NASA admitted that the film stock had probably been reused to save money – they had taped over one of the greatest moments in human history for the sake of a few dollars.

NASA was forced to dig out old copies of the original television broadcast and enlisted experts to enhance them as best they could, though the final result is not quite as clear as it might have been.

TOWERING ERROR

DATE: 1173

In the late twelfth century, the wealthy trading city of Pisa, Italy, broke ground with the construction of a 60-metre-high tower to house the great bells of the Piazza dei Miracoli cathedral. It was to be one of the finest structures in Europe, but instead became the Continent's most famous folly – in both senses of the word. The Pisan soil was too soft for the tower's shallow foundations, meaning that the structure was already tilting to the north by the time the second storey was built. By then it was probably too late to rectify, and so they carried on with the construction. Two hundred years later, the bell tower was complete. Thanks to a recent restoration project to help tilt the tower back the other way, it is claimed that the tower should remain standing for at least another 300 years. The true wonder of this building is that it's still standing.

 **DID YOU KNOW?**

In 1934, Benito Mussolini decided that the Tower of Pisa was contrary to his country's new fascist architecture of straight lines and right angles. The dictator ordered engineers to pump cement under the building to reverse its tilt, but hundreds of tonnes of concrete only succeeded in making the tower even more lopsided.

7

ACADEMY A-FLAWED

The scene: The 2017 Oscars.

The players: Hollywood legends Warren Beatty and Faye Dunaway.

The role: Announcing the Best Picture winner, the most important prize-giving of the night.

BEATTY: "... and the Academy Award, for Best Picture..."

[Beatty hands the envelope to Dunaway for extra dramatic tension – or perhaps because he appears confused by what is written on the card]

DUNAWAY: "*La La Land!*"

And we are imagining this scene because...? It was not the right answer.

Beatty had been given an envelope declaring the winner of the Best Actress award, *La La Land*'s Emma Stone, not Best Picture. He looked confused because he was; he wondered why Stone's name was on the card. The error was revealed after Oscars staff hurried on stage, and *La La Land* producer Fred Berger finished his speech with the words, "We lost, by the way," before the real winner – *Moonlight* – was declared.

THE MYSPACE MISTAKE

DATE: 2005

If you're of a certain age you might remember a social media website called Myspace, which was hugely popular for a time in the 2000s. In July 2005, media mogul Rupert Murdoch's News Corp bought the two-year-old company for $580 million. One year later, the company was valued at $1.5 billion and had overtaken Google as the most popular site in the United States. It was ten times as popular as Facebook.

In 2012, however, News Corp made the painful decision to offload Myspace for a pitiful $35 million, just 6 per cent of what it had paid for it six years earlier. Murdoch later said that Myspace had been a "huge mistake" and that his company had "mismanaged it in every possible way". That same year, Facebook floated on the stock market, valued at more than $100 billion.

FLIGHT FIGHT

DATE: 1994

The Canadian pilot and South Korean co-pilot of a Korean Air jet carrying 152 passengers were blamed after the aircraft skidded off the runway while landing in Cheju, South Korea, in high winds and rain. The Airbus A300 crashed and burst into flames, but fortunately everybody on board survived by sliding down an escape chute.

It emerged that the two pilots had argued over whether or not to abort the landing, and physically fought over the controls in the cockpit before the plane rammed into a safety barrier. Understandably, both were charged with negligence.

FLYING MAMMAL MUNITIONS

DATE: 1943

After the Japanese attack on Pearl Harbor in December 1941, dentist and part-time inventor Lytle S. Adams of Pennsylvania devised a method of revenge that the Japanese would never have seen coming.

His plan was to fix miniature incendiary charges with timers to Mexican free-tailed bats, let them loose over Japanese cities, stand back as the bats roosted in buildings, then wait for the unfortunate creatures to ignite, causing chaos. Incredibly, the government took Adams' plans seriously, and the US Army began trialling "Project X-Ray". Being wild animals with no concept of war, the bats did not follow orders. One day, a gang of explosive bats destroyed a military hangar and a general's car after being accidentally released.

Testing continued nonetheless, and Project X-Ray was not cancelled until a staggering $2 million had been spent on the venture.

THE UNWANTED WIZARD

DATE: 1995

No fewer than 12 publishers rejected *Harry Potter and the Philosopher's Stone*, the first book in J. K. Rowling's mega-selling children's series, before Bloomsbury opted to publish it in 1997.

Various reasons were given for turning down the future record-breaker after Rowling originally pitched it in 1995: it was too long; the first chapter was slow to start; the initial characters were unlikeable; the setting of a boarding school was too exclusive. Bloomsbury boss Nigel Newton was apparently also hesitant, and only decided to publish the book after his daughter read the opening chapters and pestered him to find out what happened next.

 **DID YOU KNOW?**

When J. K. Rowling turned her hand to crime novels with *The Cuckoo's Calling*, the author adopted the pseudonym Robert Galbraith – supposedly a former soldier – and pitched to publishers anonymously. Rowling shared some of Galbraith's rejection letters on social media, revealing that one even suggested a writing course. The editor of at least one large publishing house was later forced to admit embarrassment at turning down a manuscript by the world's best-selling children's writer.

TRAGIC TANKER

DATE: 24 MARCH 1989

The 240,000-tonne *Exxon Valdez* oil tanker was en route from Valdez, Alaska, to California when it encountered icebergs in the shipping lanes. As a safety precaution, Captain Joseph Hazelwood directed the vessel off course, closer to the coast, and retired to his bunk, leaving the ship's third mate – tired and unqualified – at the helm.

The tanker hit a reef at 12.04 a.m., spilling 9 million gallons of oil in a slick that eventually covered 11,000 miles of ocean and contaminated 1,300 miles of Alaskan coastline. A quarter of a million seabirds and thousands of marine mammals died as a result. The captain, who admitted to drinking vodka in a bar hours before going to sea, was given a $50,000 fine and community service, and the disaster cost the ship's operator Exxon more than $4 billion.

DOCTOR WHERE?

In today's connected world, where everything is stored in the "cloud" forever, it's hard to believe that something as valuable as a popular BBC television show, loved by millions, could be lost.

However, in the 1960s and 1970s, the BBC routinely reused original master tapes to save money and space. Tape was expensive, and old black-and-white recordings were not considered worth keeping. That's exactly how no fewer than 97 episodes of *Doctor Who* were lost – either taped over or left to deteriorate to an unwatchable state. Some episodes have been recovered from foreign broadcasters, but most are probably lost forever; unless a certain Doctor can go back in time and find them.

 **DID YOU KNOW?**

In June 1966, The Beatles made their first – and only – live appearance on *Top of the Pops*, performing "Paperback Writer" and "Rain". In the early 2000s, the BBC revealed that the tape had been wiped in the 1970s, along with 3,500 other live performances of stars such as Bob Dylan and The Rolling Stones.

KINDLING A FRIENDSHIP

DATE: 1835

The Scottish historian Thomas Carlyle gave his friend the philosopher John Stuart Mill the first volume of his *The French Revolution: A History*, his only copy, for his input. When Mill later appeared at his door, it was not useful feedback he had to offer. Instead, he had the awkward task of telling Carlyle that his maid had used the manuscript to start a fire, thinking it was waste paper.

The historian did not give up, however, and rewrote the entire volume. When it was finally published in 1837, the three-volume work made Carlyle's name.

PRODUCT MISPLACEMENT

DATE: 1982

Unbelievably, confectionary company Mars Inc. turned down an offer for their M&M's sweets to be featured in the 1982 film *E.T. the Extra-Terrestrial*, leaving Hershey Foods Corporation to take the opportunity to promote Reese's Pieces, a less popular peanut-butter-filled alternative.

Perhaps Mars felt that being associated with an alien being would not help sales? Even Hershey took some convincing; the deal was only signed after an executive visited the film studios and saw how cute E.T. was. In the film, the young hero Elliott leaves Reese's Pieces in the woods, hoping to lure E.T. into his home. It worked for him, and within weeks of the film's release in December 1982, sales of Reese's Pieces tripled.

PATENTLY STUPID

DATE: 1876

When Scottish-born American inventor Alexander Graham Bell secured a patent for the telephone, his triumph was disputed by rival inventors, and the ensuing legal battles cost him so much that he offered to sell his revolutionary creation to Western Union for $100,000. The telegraph company declined on the grounds that while the telephone was "a very interesting novelty, we have come to the conclusion that it has no commercial possibilities".

Bell set up the Bell Telephone Company instead, which was soon turning a healthy profit. Western Union quickly saw the folly of their decision and went into direct competition with Bell, but after he defeated them in court, his company dominated the US telephone business for decades to come.

 DID YOU KNOW?

It was Alexander Graham Bell's opinion that people ought to answer the telephone with the words "Ahoy-hoy!" and always did so himself. Unlike his new-fangled creation, it did not catch on. His rival, Thomas Edison, is credited with popularizing "Hello" as an alternative.

FIRE SALE

In the eighteenth century, Alaska belonged to Russia. Siberian settlers claimed the area for fur trading, particularly in lucrative sea otter pelts. By the nineteenth century, the otters were all but wiped out, and Russia needed money after losing the Crimean War.

Czar Alexander II worried that the region could easily be lost to Britain or the US with no compensation (fewer than 1,000 Russian trappers had no hope of defending a territory seven times bigger than the UK), so he decided to sell Alaska. America snapped it up for $7.2 million ($100 million today), officially taking control in October 1867. Near the end of that century, gold was discovered in the area, and the twentieth century saw a boom in oil exploration, leaving some Russians regretting losing out so greatly to a country that was to become their arch-enemy.

WINTER IS COMING

DATE: 1812

In the summer of 1812, the French Emperor Napoleon Bonaparte marched on Russia with more than 400,000 men. He met little resistance, but the retreating Russians burned villages and fields, causing serious supply problems.

Napoleon, who had been expecting a quick victory and Russian surrender, had not brought enough food to feed his men. When the French entered Moscow in September, they found it abandoned and burned, but still the Russians did not surrender. Napoleon had no option but to make a humiliating retreat through the Russian winter in temperatures as low as −30°C. He had already lost more than half his troops to disease and desertion, and the rest were devastated by hunger, Russian attacks and hypothermia. To make matters worse, his horses wore summer shoes, not fit for the freezing conditions, leaving supply waggons useless.

By the time Napoleon's "Grand Army" made it to Poland in late November that same year, it had shrunk to just 10,000 active soldiers. It would be the beginning of the end for the military mastermind.

OPERATION FREEZING NAZIS

DATE: 1941

More than a century after Napoleon's defeat, another megalomaniac with a large army at his disposal invaded Russia – Adolf Hitler. And he too fell foul of the Siberian winter.

Operation Barbarossa foundered when the overstretched Germans reached Moscow, just as the French plan failed. Like Napoleon, the Germans were expecting a quick victory and came unprepared for the Russian winter. Severely weakened by hunger and frostbite, the Nazis were driven back by the Russian Red Army. In 1943 they were defeated at the Battle of Stalingrad, which many historians see as a turning point in World War Two.

TREE TOPPED

DATE: 2011

In 2011, the Burnside Village shopping centre in Adelaide, Australia – also the site of a precious hundred-year-old river red gum tree – was set to be redeveloped. Rather than removing the ancient 18-metre-high tree, the developers decided to encase it under a glass ceiling. The radical move was criticized by, well, everyone who knew anything about trees, who warned that the tree would not be able to survive inside; it was not a houseplant. Nevertheless, $5 million was spent on measures to keep it alive.

A year later, the tree began to show signs of ill health. The management spent hundreds of thousands of dollars installing special lighting and a "misting system" to help make the organism feel more at home, and injected it with nutrients, but of course their efforts failed. In 2013, the river red gum tree was put out of its misery.

BAD VIBRATIONS

DATE: 1969

The American group the Beach Boys might be one of the most famous bands in pop history, but in 1969 they were in serious financial trouble, and it seemed as if they might be forgotten. Their biggest song, "Good Vibrations", had been a hit, but three years later they found themselves mired in a legal battle with their label, with all their energy and resources going into the dispute. As a result, it was The Beatles and The Rolling Stones who were ruling the airwaves.

Murry Wilson, father of the band's songwriter Brian and his brothers Dennis and Carl, had sold the publishing rights to their songs for $750,000, something which the band was naturally somewhat upset about. It was a lot of money at the time, but of course the decision only made the band's future financial difficulties worse; it's estimated that the rights to their songs have generated more than $100 million since the year they were sold.

HELLO?

DATE: 1962

In 1962, Dick Rowe, the top A&R man at Decca Records in the US, heard a performance by a new band from Liverpool called The Beatles. He declined to offer them a record contract, telling their manager, Brian Epstein, that he didn't like their sound, and that "guitar bands are on their way out".

Decca opted for Brian Poole and the Tremeloes instead (exactly). The Beatles signed with EMI-Parlophone, and the rest is history.

GALACTIC GAMBLE

American communications company Iridium thought it was onto a winner when it chose to develop handheld satellite phones in an age where mobile technology was really taking off. But it seems it backed the wrong horse.

With the simultaneous rise of multi-function mobile phones, there was soon little demand for something so one-dimensional as a satellite phone. The company's mere 55,000 users were not even enough to cover its interest repayments, and as such, it entered bankruptcy just nine months after it was founded, not least because it had already spent more than $5 billion on launching 88 satellites into space.

The satellites were set to burn up in Earth's atmosphere, but at the last minute they were saved by investors who, with the help of the US government, bought them for a snip at $35 million.

MELTDOWN MADNESS

The tsunami that hit the east coast of Japan in 2011 was devastating. Its biggest impact was arguably that felt at the Fukushima Daiichi nuclear power station, where the electricity supply was destroyed, along with all but one of its back-up generators. With no working cooling system, three nuclear reactors went into meltdown, causing explosions and releasing radioactive material. The resulting fallout forced 150,000 people to evacuate their homes.

After the disaster, investigators found that opportunities had been missed to correct flaws that rendered the power station vulnerable to flooding: Fukushima was built too low on the coast; the seawalls were not high enough; the builders and operators fatally underestimated the size of possible tidal waves – ignoring warnings from their own experts; the back-up generators were lying too low.

A 2015 study concluded that "Fukushima Daiichi was a sitting duck waiting to be flooded".

UP IN SMOKE

John Warburton was a herald of arms, antiquarian and mapmaker, as well as an avid – if clumsy – collector of old books and manuscripts. One day, he left a pile of sixteenth- and seventeenth-century original drama scripts in his kitchen, and proceeded to forget about them for an entire year. When he came looking for the papers, he discovered, to his horror, that his cook had used them all for lighting fires.

A surviving scrap of paper lists the collection, which consisted of work by playwrights such as Christopher Marlowe; scripts performed by the King's Men, Shakespeare's theatre company; and even original Shakespeare manuscripts – including what may have been an early version of *Henry IV, Part II*, an unknown play called *Henry I* and the mysteriously titled *Play by Will Shakespeare*.

DID YOU KNOW?

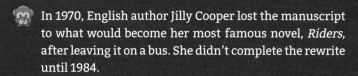 In 1970, English author Jilly Cooper lost the manuscript to what would become her most famous novel, *Riders*, after leaving it on a bus. She didn't complete the rewrite until 1984.

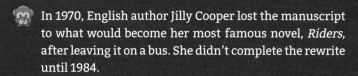 The Russian writer Nikolai Gogol spent years writing the second part of his novel *Dead Souls* (the first part of which was published to acclaim in 1842), then burned it on a stove after falling under the influence of an eccentric religious mystic. He blamed evil spirits for the error.

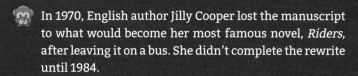 In the 1970s, Nobel Laureate V. S. Naipaul put a collection of unpublished novels, manuscripts, letters and diaries into storage in a London warehouse. Twenty years later, he discovered that the materials had been accidentally incinerated.

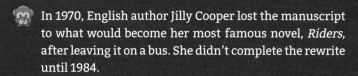 Edna St Vincent Millay, a Pulitzer Prize-winning American poet, took the manuscript for *Conversation at Midnight*, which she had been planning for years, on holiday with her to Florida in 1936. When her hotel went up in flames, taking her poetry with it, Millay rewrote the book from memory and it was published the following year.

MURAL MISTAKE

The Spanish artist Cecilia Giménez's work made headlines for all the wrong reasons in August 2012. The 80-year-old painter made an effort to restore *Ecce Homo*, a faded fresco of Jesus on the walls of a church in Borja, but she got a bit carried away with her brushes. The finished image bore so little resemblance to the original that it was dubbed the "worst restoration in history", drawing not only widespread derision from around the world but also hundreds of thousands of new visitors to the church.

Giménez felt the reaction was unfair as she had been unable to complete the restoration before going on holiday. If only she could have finished the job, the whole fuss would have been avoided. It's more likely, perhaps, that her vacation saved *Ecce Homo* from further artistic indignity.

It wasn't all bad news for Cecilia, though. After she became famous around the world for her botched restoration, the amateur artist was able to command far more money for her previously obscure paintings. And the hordes of visitors who flocked to see the faulty fresco brought in much-needed funds for the church.

MISTAKEN MEMORIAL

DATE: 1977

In 1977, a statue was erected in Stockton-on-Tees, UK, to commemorate the nineteenth-century chemist John Walker, a local hero. Unlike most famous statues, the sculpture of the town's favourite son cannot be found in the town square or some other prominent location. Walker was originally given pride of place in the town's high street, but after a few months he was hidden away in a corner of a shopping centre.

In 2016, the reason for this odd placement was revealed: the figure was not the fabled inventor of the friction matchstick, but an actor of the same period also called John Walker, who had never even been to Stockton-on-Tees. Other attempts to commemorate Walker in the town have also failed: a plastic sculpture of a match installed in 2001 proved so unpopular with locals that it was removed.

CAN YOU FILL ME IN?

DATE: JULY 2016

Reading-work-piece is an artwork from 1965 created by the German artist Arthur Köpcke, consisting of an empty crossword puzzle. At least it used to be empty.

An elderly visitor to the Nuremberg museum where the work was on display mistook the €80,000 piece for an interactive exhibit – to be fair, it does say "insert words" in English on it – and filled in some of the clues with a pen. The doodler was investigated for criminal damage, but she responded that the museum should have seen it coming, because there was no notice telling visitors not to draw on the artwork.

EXPENSIVE ELBOW

DATE: 2006

The casino mogul and art collector Steve Wynn had arranged a deal to sell *Le Rêve*, a 1932 oil painting by Pablo Picasso, for $139 million. It would be the most expensive art sale in history.

A few days before money was to change hands, Wynn hosted a group of friends and showed them the painting. Wynn suffered from a condition that affected his peripheral vision, and as he talked about the artwork, he was unaware of how close he was to it. As he stepped back, he put his elbow through the painting, tearing a 6-inch hole in the canvas. Needless to say, the deal was off. Seven years and one expensive repair job later, Wynn did eventually sell *Le Rêve* to the buyer he had previously lined up.

 DID YOU KNOW?

In 2015, staff at the Egyptian Museum in Cairo managed to break the famous beard on the priceless 3,000-year-old gold death mask of the Pharaoh Tutankhamun. They then botched the repair by using an unsightly epoxy glue.

CONTROVERSIAL CARVING

DATE: 1948

When Polish-American artist Korczak Ziolkowski began work on a giant rock sculpture of the Native American Crazy Horse, he probably knew that he wouldn't finish it. The memorial, carved into the Black Hills of South Dakota, depicts the legendary Sioux chief on horseback. At the time of writing it is still unfinished, but if it is ever completed the sculpture will stand more than 560 feet high, taller than Mount Rushmore, and extend 640 feet out.

If things follow plan, Crazy Horse's left arm will be outstretched over his horse's head, his index finger pointing to the lands of his tribe. Unfortunately, in traditional Native American culture, pointing with a single finger is regarded as a confrontational gesture. It's plain rude. As the hand is expected to be 25 feet tall, that will probably be noticed. It's also controversial because some modern descendants of Crazy Horse believe that carving a huge image into the hills is a desecration of their burial grounds.

FLOATING FOLLY

DATE: 1940

In August 1940, the Japanese Navy launched the warship *Yamato*, one of the largest battleships ever constructed, at 839 feet long and weighing 63,000 tonnes. She was designed as the ultimate battleship, "unsinkable", with among the largest guns ever fitted to a warship.

Yamato took three years to build, and by the time she was launched, she was obsolete. Ship-on-ship fights were no longer necessary, as aircraft carriers could launch warplanes out of range of enemy shells. When Japan entered World War Two in 1941, *Yamato* spent much of the conflict confined to port: a huge grey elephant. She fired her giant guns against enemy ships only once.

In 1945, the struggling Japanese Navy finally put her into action against the Americans, but she was overwhelmed by an aerial attack and sank after a spectacular explosion, taking 2,500 crew with her.

STAR FLAWS

When film companies finance new films, they generally try to ensure as much profit as possible, but when George Lucas secured funding from 20th Century Fox to make his first *Star Wars* movie, he asked for a relatively small fee to write and direct the film in return for ownership of the *Star Wars* idea. Fox agreed, allowing Lucas to retain all rights to the merchandizing, characters and follow-ups after two years.

The huge success of *Star Wars* that ensued, in sequels, toys and modern spin-offs, meant that Fox effectively signed away billions of dollars in future income. "Nobody will admit to being the person at Fox who let this deal happen," said the lawyer who helped secure the deal for Lucas. The filmmaker is now worth about $5 billion.

 DID YOU KNOW?

Both Universal and United Artists rejected *Star Wars* before 20th Century Fox agreed to make the film. The directors of *The Exorcist* and *The Godfather*, William Friedkin and Francis Ford Coppola respectively, also turned down a chance to produce it.

#FAIL

The launch party for one of singer Susan Boyle's new albums was promoted on Twitter with the announcement that the Scottish star would be hosting an exclusive album-listening party for fans. The event was promoted with the hashtag #susanalbumparty.

It was hastily deleted, and you can figure out why for yourself.

CANNED OPPORTUNITIES

Pepsi versus Coca-Cola is one of the twentieth century's most famous business rivalries. But Coca-Cola could have nipped it in the bud not once, but twice.

Pepsi-Cola was created in 1893 by the pharmacist Caleb Bradham, but in 1922 the company went bankrupt after speculating on volatile sugar prices. Bradham offered to sell the company to Coca-Cola, but they turned him down.

A Wall Street investor took over the ailing drinks maker, but by 1931 Pepsi was on the verge of a second bankruptcy and again offered to Coca-Cola. Once more they declined. This time Pepsi was taken over by Charles Guth, a retail magnate with a grudge against Coca-Cola. Guth changed the Pepsi recipe to emulate Coca-Cola, and under his guidance the company became Coca-Cola's biggest competitor in only a few years.

GOOGLE THAT

In 1999, the Internet businessman George Bell, owner of Excite, passed up on an opportunity to buy a young search engine called Google for just $1 million. Bell baulked at a part of the deal that required Excite to replace its search technology with Google's. The price was reduced to $750,000, but still he refused.

At the time of writing, Google's market capitalization is more than $800 billion. Bell has since said that "I think the decision we made at the time... was a good decision. It's laughable to say that now, I suppose."

APPLE ANGST

Ronald Wayne was an early shareholder in US technology giant Apple with Steve Jobs and Steve Wozniak. Forty-something Wayne was brought in as a responsible adult to oversee the young co-founders and organize documentation. But Wayne quickly became worried that he could be saddled with the company's debt, so he sold his 10 per cent share after just 12 days for $800.

Today that stake would be worth almost $100 billion, making him one of the richest people in the world. But he claims not to regret his decision. He does, however, regret selling the original contract he signed with Apple for $500 in the 1990s. That same document sold for $1.6 million in 2011.

LOSING TRACK

DATE: 2014

In 2014, it was revealed that 2,000 new trains ordered by the French rail operator RFF from train company SNCF were too big; they were too wide to fit into train stations. Having spent €15 billion on the larger locomotives, the operator had no choice but to spend at least €50 million on adjusting the platforms at more than a thousand regional train stations.

The error occurred after RFF neglected to tell SNCF about old train platforms built to accommodate slimmer trains from 50 years ago, and SNCF failed to check the measurements.

It was later discovered that SNCF's new trains were also too tall to fit through Italian tunnels on their proposed European Riviera coastal route. Instead, the trains travel as far as the French border and passengers disembark for an Italian service.

TITANIC COCK-UPS

DATE: 15 APRIL 1912

A litany of errors contributed to the deaths of more than 1,500 people when the "unsinkable" liner *Titanic* sank. Before she set sail, the vessel's operator J. Bruce Ismay ordered that the number of lifeboats be reduced from 48 to 20 (14 standard ones, two cutters, plus four folding boats) – the figure legally required by ships four times smaller, and enough for only half of the ship's 2,200 passengers.

In the lead-up to the collision with the iceberg, the ship's radio operators neglected to relay several of the iceberg warnings they had received to the crew in charge. Two lookouts in the *Titanic*'s crow's nest did not even have binoculars. Captain Edward Smith knew that the ship was heading for an iceberg zone; nevertheless, he did not order a change of course or reduce the ship's speed from a maximum 22.5 knots. Instead, he went to dinner, leaving the controls in the hands of the first officer.

DID YOU KNOW?

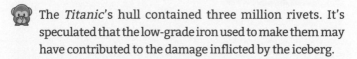

The *Titanic*'s hull contained three million rivets. It's speculated that the low-grade iron used to make them may have contributed to the damage inflicted by the iceberg.

The *Titanic* had only spent a few hours in sea trials before her maiden voyage from Southampton, UK, to New York, and had never been helmed at full speed.

Thomas Andrews, the ship's naval architect, remained in the first-class smoking room, resigned to his fate, while the "unsinkable" liner sank.

American mining tycoon Benjamin Guggenheim and his valet changed into full evening dress when he realized he would not survive. He's reported to have said: "We've dressed up in our best and are prepared to go down like gentlemen."

Twenty-two crew members missed the voyage. Three brothers hired to work in the ship's coal bunkers stopped for a drink in a pub en route, and failed to board after being delayed by a passing train.

Titanic passenger John Jacob Astor IV was one of the richest men in the world, worth around $100 million. He did not survive.

ALEXANDER THE GREAT?

DATE: 323 BC

Alexander the Great was king of Macedonia in the fourth century BC. He united the Greek city-states and conquered much of Asia, including Persia and Babylon (modern-day Iraq) where he died at the age of 32. His empire wouldn't have lasted forever, but Alexander didn't help much with the estate planning.

Although he had an unborn son, Alexander did not nominate him as his heir, instead letting it be known that he should be succeeded only by the "strongest". After he died, his huge empire split among his four strongest generals – one of whom went on to kill the late king's young son, wife and mother – who ruled over warring dynasties for decades.

METRIC MARS MISSION

DATE: SEPTEMBER 1999

In December 1998, NASA launched the Mars Climate Orbiter on a long journey to Mars, where it was to orbit the planet and relay data from another mission back to Earth. Ten months later, on the day when the spacecraft was supposed to enter Mars' orbit, it disappeared from the screens at Mission Control. Something had clearly gone wrong with the navigation.

It turned out that one team of engineers had calculated the required navigation using metric units, while another used imperial. That was all it took for the $195 million spaceship to stray too close to the Red Planet and burn up in its atmosphere.

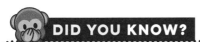

DID YOU KNOW?

The billion-dollar Mars Observer spacecraft was launched in 1992 to study the Red Planet's geography. Three days before it was to enter Mars' orbit it disappeared. What happened to this spacecraft remains a mystery.

MISSION OUT OF CONTROL

NASA's Genesis spacecraft was launched in August 2001. It travelled toward the Sun to collect samples of solar wind. In September 2004, Genesis returned to Earth, having travelled 20 million miles, to drop off a capsule containing the valuable samples.

The plan was that a parachute would allow the capsule to be safely picked up by a helicopter. Unfortunately, the canopy failed to open, leaving the pod to crash-land in the Utah desert at 100 mph, ripping open the canister containing the solar samples. Luckily, some of the samples were salvageable. It was later revealed that the capsule's gravity switches, designed to release the parachute, had been installed backward.

ALWAYS CHECK YOUR WORK

DATE: 1962

Mariner 1 was the United States' first interplanetary probe, designed to conduct a flyby of the planet Venus to collect scientific data. Sadly, Mariner veered dangerously off course shortly after take-off on 22 July, and NASA Mission Control was forced to abort the mission after only five minutes, ditching the $18 million spacecraft into the sea just seconds before control would have been lost.

An investigation revealed that the error was caused by a single missing "overbar" (like a hyphen) in the navigational computer code.

TERRIBLE TYPO

DATE: 2008

The Chilean mint was left with egg on its face after the country's name was spelled "C-h-i-i-e" on its 50-peso coins. Incredibly, the howler went unnoticed for more than a year, during which time thousands of the coins were produced.

The general manager of the mint and several other employees were dismissed over the error, but the coins were not taken out of circulation, and they are now collectors' items.

AMERICA THIRST

The eighteenth amendment to the United States constitution declared, "the manufacture, sale, or transportation of intoxicating liquors... for beverage purposes is hereby prohibited." America was now dry. But Americans did not turn into teetotallers. Instead, the law drove alcohol underground and organized crime thrived, making the fortunes of gangsters like Al Capone.

A black market of bootleggers supplied illicit "speakeasy" bars with smuggled foreign booze – usually hard liquor, which was more profitable than beer. Illegal distilling was rife, and people died after drinking lethal "moonshine" they had made in their own bathtubs.

In 1921, the law was eased, allowing alcohol use for medical purposes, leading to a spike in doctor's visits. In 1933, the booze ban became the only US constitutional amendment ever to be repealed.

ERRONEOUS ENSIGN

DATE: 1889

Why did a Caribbean island have an igloo on its flag for 80 years? The Turks and Caicos Islands, a British territory in the Caribbean, is known for its white sandy beaches and salt ponds. The islanders would rake the valuable mineral into large salt mounds for collection, an image of which is included on the island's official seal.

In the late nineteenth century the seal was incorporated into a new flag for the islands, to be produced back in England. The designer, presumably not a well-travelled individual, mistook the piles of salt for igloos – in the Caribbean?! – and added a door. The egregious error was not flagged up until 1967.

BONE HEADS

The American palaeontologists Othniel Marsh and Edward Cope were locked in a bitter rivalry toward the end of the nineteenth century, with each seeking to identify the most dinosaurs. Their competition led to the "discovery" of one of the most famous prehistoric creatures – but it never actually existed.

In 1877, Marsh found the skeleton of a long-necked dinosaur that he named Apatosaurus. Two years later, fossil collectors sent him the bones of another similar reptile. In his rush to beat Cope, Marsh declared it to be another new species, Brontosaurus, meaning "Thunder Lizard", but it was actually another Apatosaurus. Although the error was eventually exposed, the idea of Brontosaurus proved hard to kill off. Even the prestigious Carnegie Museum in Pittsburgh exhibited an Apatosaurus as a Brontosaurus until 1979.

 **DID YOU KNOW?**

Marsh and Cope laid claim to 142 new species between them, during what became known as the "Bone Wars", but today only about 30 of their dinosaur discoveries are considered genuine.

DINO-FLAWS

A film about an island on which recently reborn prehistoric dinosaurs run riot was never going to be entirely factual, but *Jurassic Park* (1993) had some serious palaeontological issues.

The star of the picture, *Tyrannosaurus rex*, was not even alive during the Jurassic period; the predator evolved tens of millions of years later in the Cretaceous, along with Triceratops, another species featured in the film.

The fearsome Velociraptors, of the famous kitchen scene, were not only millions of years out of context – they too were from the Cretaceous – but also not terribly fearsome in real life. They were barely 2 feet high and covered in feathers, possibly resembling a vicious turkey. The intelligence they display in the film is also highly exaggerated, as they were actually no smarter than your average wildfowl.

RED LIGHT = DANGER

DATE: 1868

In 1868, the world's first traffic lights were trialled outside the Houses of Parliament in England. The lights were the brainchild of English railway engineer John Peake Knight, who thought that train signalling systems could be put to use to manage horse-drawn carriage traffic in London's streets.

The manually operated lights were initially regarded as a success, and more were planned, until one month into the experiment the gas-powered lamps exploded, badly injuring the policeman operating them. The idea was scrapped as a result, and traffic lights would not return to London for another 60 years.

DID YOU KNOW?

 In January 2000, Internet giant AOL absorbed media company Time Warner in a deal worth $360 billion. Three years later, the company posted a record $100 billion loss, and the two split in 2009, with AOL worth just $2.5 billion.

 In 2009, ITV sold Friends Reunited for £25 million after paying £175 million for the website four years earlier.

 The Quaker Oats Company bought juice brand Snapple in 1994 for $1.7 billion. Three years later Quaker sold Snapple for just $300 million. The chairman and president of Quaker both left their jobs as a consequence. Snapple survived and three years later was sold for $1 billion.

RADIUM GIRLS

DATE: 1920s

In early twentieth-century America, the highly radioactive element radium was used in luminous paints for clock faces and wristwatches. The job of painting the dials was largely carried out by young women: so-called "Radium Girls".

They were instructed to lick their brushes, so that they could paint more accurately, and so were regularly ingesting radioactive material. The safety risks were not understood at the time; radium was actually thought to be healthy! Workers would use the glow-in-the-dark paint on their faces for fun, but over time they suffered from anaemia, toothache and broken bones. Young women died of necrosis of the jaw and bone cancer.

Eventually, a group of radium girls brought legal action and the dangerous practices were stopped, but radium paint was still used in watches until 1968, and some of the factory sites are radioactive to this day.

SICK SHIP

DATE: 1875

The SS *Bessemer* was a ship invented to cure seasickness. The vessel was designed and built by the English inventor Sir Henry Bessemer, who suffered terribly from the condition. The *Bessemer* was a 350-foot-long paddle steamer that featured a swinging cabin designed to remain level while the ship was at sea.

Tests in port were promising, and on 8 May 1875 she set sail on her maiden voyage from Dover to Calais with hundreds of people aboard. But the swinging saloon did not work. If the sea was calm, it didn't move; if it was rough, it didn't remain level. And that wasn't the only problem: the *Bessemer* was too large for French ports, and she proved impossible to control at low speeds.

When the ship docked at Calais it demolished the pier. Sir Henry's expensive vessel never sailed again and was eventually sold for scrap.

NO FEAR OF MISSING OUT

American actor Steve McQueen is famous for his cool-customer persona in classic films such as *The Great Escape* (1963) and *Bullitt* (1968). But the actor might have had a larger role in Hollywood history if he hadn't been so picky. He turned down parts in such iconic films as *Ocean's 11* (1960), *Breakfast at Tiffany's* (1961), *Dirty Harry* (1971), *The French Connection* (1971) – a role for which Gene Hackman won an Oscar – *Close Encounters of the Third Kind* (1977) and *Apocalypse Now* (1979).

Negotiations for 1969's *Butch Cassidy and the Sundance Kid* broke down after his agent demanded top billing over Paul Newman. McQueen was also rejected for the lead role in *Superman* (1978) because he was too fat.

NOT-SO-WISE WIZARD

Another celebrated actor who might have regretted snubbing a role was Scot Sir Sean Connery, who turned down the role of Gandalf in *The Lord of the Rings* trilogy because he couldn't get to grips with the complicated plot. The offer was $6 million per film plus an unprecedented 15 per cent of worldwide box office takings; a percentage that by 2018 could have netted Connery something in the region of $400 million, the highest fee ever paid to an actor.

The James Bond legend later reflected on his decision to turn down the Tolkien epic: "Yeah, well, I never understood it. I read the book, I read the script, I saw the movie. I still don't understand it."

 **DID YOU KNOW?**

It wasn't just Sir Sean who turned down a role in The Lord of the Rings blockbusters. It's been reported that Russell Crowe, Nicolas Cage, Kate Winslet, Ethan Hawke, Uma Thurman, Christopher Plummer and Daniel Day-Lewis were all approached.

DID YOU KNOW?

Cary Grant turned down the chance to play James Bond in the super-spy's first film outing *Dr. No* (1962), leaving Sean Connery to take the role that made his name.

Will Smith declined the lead role of Neo in *The Matrix* (1999) in order to make *Wild Wild West*, the best part of which was Smith's theme song.

Julia Roberts turned down the part in *Basic Instinct* that made Sharon Stone a star. Roberts had already made her name in *Pretty Woman* (1990), however, and given the nature of Stone's most famous scene in the 1992 thriller, it's understandable that Hollywood's one-time highest paid actress might have had qualms. Michelle Pfeiffer, Kim Basinger and Meg Ryan also rejected the role.

Michael Madsen turned down the role of Vincent Vega in *Pulp Fiction* (1994) because of rehearsals for *Wyatt Earp*. John Travolta got the role instead, and his acting career was resurrected.

It might be impossible to imagine these two acting legends in the role, but both Clint Eastwood and Sylvester Stallone turned down the chance to play Axel Foley in *Beverly Hills Cop* (1984), before Eddie Murphy made the character his own.

CRINGE

The "romantic comedy" *Tiptoes* (2003) was a film bad enough to destroy careers, but somehow its stars survived. Matthew McConaughey and Kate Beckinsale played Steven and Carol, a couple with the perfect life – until Steven reluctantly reveals that he is the only tall person in a family of dwarves.

Most of the cast are genuinely short people, including future *Game of Thrones* star Peter Dinklage, but the starring role of McConaughey's twin brother Rolfe was given to Gary Oldman – not especially tall at 5 feet 9 inches, but certainly not a dwarf. Oldman's part, dubbed "the role of a lifetime" by the film's makers, required the actor to walk around on his knees, while crude movie magic attempted to give the impression that he was 4 feet tall.

Despite the film's famous cast, it was never released in cinemas, and those who did see it criticized it for being tasteless, unfunny and patronizing.

ACTING UP

The 2016 fantasy-adventure film *Gods of Egypt* was criticized for selecting a largely white cast to play ancient Egyptian deities. Gerard Butler played the god Set, with a Scottish accent, and the Dane Nikolaj Coster-Waldau appeared as Horus. The film also cast white Australians Rachael Blake, Geoffrey Rush and Bryan Brown as the gods Isis, Ra and Osiris. The casting was seen as a textbook example of Hollywood "whitewashing", harking back to a time when famous white actors were crudely made up to look like ethnic minorities.

Despite an apology from director Alex Proyas, *Gods of Egypt* was hammered by critics and bombed at the box office, failing to recoup its $140 million budget after a worldwide release.

 **DID YOU KNOW?**

The epic movie *Exodus: Gods and Kings* (2014) drew fire for casting Christian Bale as Moses, Joel Edgerton as the Egyptian emperor Ramses, Sigourney Weaver as his mother Tuya and *Breaking Bad*'s Aaron Paul as Joshua. Director Ridley Scott responded that he had to cast big Hollywood names to secure funding to make the film.

MANGA MISCASTING

Casting a global star like Scarlett Johansson in a new film might not seem like a controversial choice, but the actress was criticized for taking on the role of Motoko Kusanagi in the American live-action version of the cult 1996 Japanese animation *Ghost in the Shell*.

In the original, Kusanagi is Japanese, but Johansson is clearly not. More than 100,000 people signed a petition demanding that the character be recast. Film critics were underwhelmed when the film was released in 2017, and it was a flop at the box office.

UNCONQUERED

Legendary American film producer Howard Hughes' 1956 epic *The Conqueror*, about Genghis Khan, was cursed from the start. The script was written for Marlon Brando, but he was unavailable. John Wayne chanced upon the script while visiting director Dick Powell's office, and decided that he was the man to play the twelfth-century Mongol warlord. Powell was surprised, but agreed. "Who am I to turn down John Wayne?" he later explained. It was one of the worst casting decisions ever made.

Wayne's cowboy style was completely wrong for the film's grand dialogue, especially when delivered in an American accent. To make matters worse, the Wild West icon was covered in "yellowface" make-up and had his eyes taped up to make him appear more oriental. *The Conqueror* was a flop and is renowned as one of the worst films ever made.

Unlike most people who saw the film, producer Howard Hughes was a big fan of *The Conqueror*. In the producer's later years as an eccentric recluse, it was one of the few films he watched obsessively. But he didn't want anybody else to see it, so he spent millions of dollars securing the sole rights to the film, and his private projectionist had to wear a blindfold.

DID YOU KNOW?

Many more respectable actors have been cast controversially throughout the years:

Elizabeth Taylor's most famous role was as the eponymous Egyptian queen in *Cleopatra* (1963).

Mickey Rooney's performance as Holly Golightly's Asian landlord in *Breakfast at Tiffany's* (1961) resorted to famously crude stereotypes.

Wearing heavy make-up and spending two months studying Japanese culture did not help Marlon Brando pull off the role of a Japanese interpreter for the US Navy in *The Teahouse of the August Moon* (1956).

The great Laurence Olivier blotted his copybook when he literally blacked-up to play Othello in a 1965 screen version of Shakespeare's tragedy.

Katharine Hepburn's performance as Chinese girl Jade Tan, complete with fake eyelids, in *Dragon Seed* (1944) was not well received.

MOGGIE MADNESS

DATE: 1966

In the 1960s, the CIA enlisted a cat to serve as a secret agent. Operation "Acoustic Kitty" required listening equipment to be surgically inserted inside the animal. The cat would then be trained to act as a stealth mobile bugging device directed by voice commands over radio, able to sneak up on unsuspecting surveillance targets. A transmitter was wired to the base of the cat's skull, the microphone was inserted into the ears and the antenna was woven into the hair of the tail.

In 1966, the Acoustic Kitty was sent on its first live public mission. It wasn't long before the furtive feline strayed across a road and was flattened by a taxi. Five years of planning and a $20 million investment were crushed. The bizarre experiment was only revealed in the early 2000s.

DON'T EAT THE BREAD

DATE: 1951

When hundreds of people from Pont-Saint-Esprit, France, began to suffer from sudden terrifying hallucinations and mystery illnesses, the phenomenon was blamed on bread contaminated with psychedelic fungus.

However, in 2010, journalist H. P. Albarelli Jr, who came across CIA documents pertaining to the event while investigating another story, made claims that the outbreak was caused by a clandestine mind-control experiment in which the bread was purposely spiked with LSD so that the effects could be monitored.

People were so badly affected by psychotic delusions that sufferers had to be strapped into hospital beds for their own safety – one man tried to drown himself because he thought snakes were eating him – and five people died.

INSECURITY SERVICES

DATE: 2008

When a delivery driver from Hemel Hempstead, UK, purchased a second-hand camera for £17 on an online auction site, the last thing he expected to find was images of named terror suspects, fingerprints and heavy weaponry. It's speculated that an MI6 agent sold the camera and forgot to delete top-secret surveillance snaps.

It's thought that the files related to an operation against al-Qaeda in Iraq, and included images of documents concerning highly confidential computer systems used by the security services. The buyer told his local police station about the images, leading to five visits to his home from Special Operations anti-terrorist officers.

FOOTBALL FUMBLE

The "nuclear football" is a nickname for the briefcase containing the launch codes and secure communications for an American president to launch a nuclear attack. It must remain close to the president at all times, in the hands of a military aide.

In 1999, President Clinton unwittingly left his nuclear-armed aide at a NATO meeting after hastily departing for the White House in his motorcade. Fortunately, the meeting was only four blocks away, and the aide walked back.

More worryingly, more than one former Clinton staffer has claimed that the president misplaced the card that bears the nuclear launch codes, the so-called "biscuit", for several months. Therefore, it's possible that Clinton would not have been able to launch an instant nuclear retaliation if the country had been attacked. The card was replaced and the original was never found.

DID YOU KNOW?

It's said that President Jimmy Carter once left the "biscuit" in a suit that he sent to the dry cleaners. Presidents Richard Nixon, Gerald Ford and George H.W. Bush have all been separated from the codes at some point, according to reports.

ATOMIC BUMBLE

DATE: THE COLD WAR PERIOD

The United States government lost several of its nuclear weapons at the height of tensions with the Soviet Union during the Cold War.

In 1958, a bomber armed with two such devices disappeared in bad weather in the Mediterranean. The bombs have never been recovered. In 1961, two 4-megaton nuclear weapons were dropped on North Carolina when a B-52 bomber broke up after take-off. Each bomb was 250 times more powerful than the 1945 Hiroshima explosion, but thankfully they did not detonate.

In 1968, a bomber carrying four nuclear devices crashed in Greenland. Three of the bombs ruptured, but a nuclear explosion was avoided. Nonetheless, highly radioactive material was blasted over the area. The fourth bomb is thought to be lying dormant under the ice, and it's possible that the missing warhead could still function today.

PRACTICE MAKES PERFECT?

During World War Two, a United States B-17 bomber dropped bombs on Boise City, Oklahoma. The pilots were on a training mission from a Texas air base and somehow mistook the lights in the city square for their firing range, which was 45 miles away. That's right, they bombed America. The first bomb landed just after midnight on 5 July, crashing through a garage and leaving a deep crater in the floor; the second damaged a church.

When the authorities discovered what was happening they cut all power, and the B-17 crew eventually realized their mistake, but not before dropping four more bombs. Fortunately, the bombs were relatively weak practice explosives, and nobody was injured. The incident gives Boise the dubious honour of being the only mainland US city to be bombed during the war.

BLAST-OFF

Inside an underground nuclear missile silo outside Vale, South Dakota, USA, lurked a Minuteman Intercontinental Ballistic Missile. The 65,000-lb weapon carried a thermonuclear warhead that would have caused 250,000 deaths if detonated over a US city.

One night, a pair of airmen were carrying out maintenance on the silo security system with the missile only a few feet away. One of them changed a fuse using the wrong tool, causing a short circuit that fired the missile's retrorockets – something only supposed to happen once it was in space. The blast knocked the 750-lb warhead to the bottom of the 80-foot silo, damaging the missile, and smoke filled the chamber as the airmen hurriedly evacuated.

A 2,000-foot perimeter was set up in case the missile exploded, but fortunately a nuclear disaster was avoided. Once the rockets had burned out, the warhead was lifted very, very carefully from the silo floor.

The Minuteman ICBM was designed to reach the Soviet Union within half an hour, carrying several times the explosive power of the bomb that flattened Hiroshima in 1945. Details of the "broken arrow" incident were only revealed in 2017, and an Air Force report on the emergency remains classified.

RABBIT RAMPAGE

DATE: 1859

When Thomas Austin introduced 12 pairs of rabbits onto his land in Victoria, Australia, he was only thinking about dinner. The English settler and sheep farmer explained that "the introduction of a few rabbits could do little harm and might provide a touch of home, in addition to a spot of hunting". Austin was clearly not familiar with the phrase "at it like rabbits".

Ten years later, his harmless dozen had exploded into a population of two million. The hungry bunnies tore through the local vegetation, which was unable to recover. By 1950, there were one billion rabbits in Australia, and the government was so desperate that it introduced the myxomatosis virus to cull the numbers.

The rabbits cost $200 million a year in pest control and have caused a 10 per cent decline in Australian fauna and flora since their innocent introduction.

THE GREAT LEAP BACKWARD

DATE: 1958

The "Four Pests" campaign was instigated by the Chinese leader Mao Zedong to curb disease and increase agricultural production as part of his communist revolution to strengthen the nation. The idea was to eliminate rats, mosquitoes, flies and sparrows. Yes, sparrows, because they were thought to eat large amounts of grain.

The Chinese state started a country-wide propaganda effort, encouraging both young and old to swat, shoot and catch any vermin they could find. Citizens banged pots and pans in order to keep sparrows from landing until they died from exhaustion. The campaign was highly successful; it's thought that more than one billion sparrows were vanquished.

What Mao did not foresee, however, was the effect that killing so many birds would have on the ecosystem. One billion sparrows eat a lot of insects; with those birds gone the bugs were free to feast on vital crops. The government realized its mistake, swapping birds for bedbugs in the four pests, and even imported sparrows from the Soviet Union, but the damage was done. The resulting ecological imbalance is partly blamed for the famine that hit the country in the following years.

TOP 10 WORST
BOX-OFFICE FLOPS

Film	Budget	Loss
Mars Needs Moms (2011)	$150,000,000	$110,450,242
The Adventures of Pluto Nash (2002)	$100,000,000	$92,905,005
The Nutcracker in 3D (2010)	$90,000,000	$69,533,984
The Alamo (2004)	$92,000,000	$68,088,638
The 13th Warrior (1999)	$125,000,000	$63,357,202
Monster Trucks (2017)	$125,000,000	$63,301,101
Lolita (1998)	$55,000,000	$53,852,216
Gigli (2003)	$54,000,000	$46,873,998
Titan A.E. (2000)	$75,000,000	$38,248,021
King Arthur: Legend of the Sword (2017)	$175,000,000	$35,049,292

MONEY FOR NOTHING

DATE: 2007

The United States government has produced more than one billion coins that nobody wants. In 2007, a campaign was started to get American consumers to use one-dollar coins instead of their favoured paper bills. The programme was due to continue until 2016, but was shut down in 2011, when the Treasury realized that nobody was using them.

The Federal Reserve still hoards around 1.2 billion dollars in change lying unwanted in their vault – in fact, more than half of all one-dollar coins ever minted are still held by the government. It's thought that the cost of making the useless coins totals more than $300 million.

The government wanted people to use coins over paper bills because, although coins are more costly to make, they last six times longer than the paper equivalent. It's estimated that swapping to metal dollars would save the government more than $4 billion over 30 years, the average life of a coin.

RISKY BUSINESS

DATE: 2008

A young derivatives trader at French bank Société Générale was convicted of forgery and "breach of trust" after getting in over his head making secret trades.

Between 2006 and 2008, Jérôme Kerviel made €50 billion of unapproved bets on the futures markets with the bank's money. At one point, Kerviel's high-risk strategy – he did not "hedge" his trades by taking opposite positions – saw him over €1 billion in profit, but like a true gambler he didn't know when to stop, and by the time he did, he had lost nearly €5 billion.

In 2010, he was sentenced to three years in jail and fined a sum equivalent to his losses.

HOW TO BREAK A BANK

Nick Leeson was a successful financial trader working for Barings Bank in Singapore. In 1993, he single-handedly accounted for 10 per cent of the 200-year-old bank's annual profit. Just two years later, the "rogue trader" had caused the collapse of Britain's oldest merchant bank after gigantically unsuccessful trades on the Asian futures markets.

Because of a company loophole, Leeson was able to hide his losses in a secret file. He chased his losses with increasingly bigger bets, until his secret account was in the red to the tune of £827 million. He was sentenced to six and a half years in a Singapore jail for fraud and forgery, and in 1995 Barings was sold to the Dutch bank ING for £1.

DID YOU KNOW?

 Morgan Stanley bond trader Howie Hubler suffered the largest single trading loss in history after making big investments in complicated financial instruments linked to the housing market. When the subprime mortgage market collapsed in 2007, his trades cost his employer $9 billion.

 Kweku Adoboli was in charge of a London trading desk for the bank UBS. What his employer didn't know was that he was taking unauthorized high-risk trades with the bank's money. He got away with it for three years, but in 2011 UBS discovered losses amounting to £1.5 billion. The bank's value plummeted by £3 billion and the chief executive resigned. In 2012, Adoboli was sentenced to seven years in jail.

 Metals trader Yasuo Hamanaka was sentenced to eight years in prison after losing $2.6 billion trying to corner the market in copper in 1996.

 Orange County, California, was declared bankrupt in 1994 after its treasurer invested public money in high-risk financial instruments. When interest rates rose, the county lost $1.7 billion, the largest such public loss ever in US history.

MAD SHEEP DISEASE

DATE: 1990s

In 1997, the Institute for Animal Health in Edinburgh, UK, received £200,000 in funding from the government to conduct research into sheep brains to see whether "mad cow disease", or BSE, had made the jump from cattle, a potentially important line of investigation.

Four years later, it emerged that scientists at the institute had been working with the wrong brains all along, using samples from cattle, not sheep. The mix-up was caused by thousands of mislabelled brain samples used in previous research. The research project collapsed, and a valuable archive of samples was lost. To this day, the question of whether sheep can contract BSE remains unanswered.

THE FÜHRER'S FAKES

On 24 April 1983, *The Sunday Times* published what might have been the scoop of the century. A German antiques dealer, Konrad Kujau, had found 60 volumes of Adolf Hitler's personal diaries. *The Sunday Times* and *The Times* spent £600,000 on the rights to serialize the journals, enlisting the help of an esteemed historian, Hugh Trevor-Roper, who examined the diaries in a Swiss bank vault and declared that they were genuine.

The Sunday Times published a six-page exclusive on the diaries, but not everybody was convinced. When the diaries were forensically examined, they were found to be old notebooks stained with tea, written using modern ink. The editor of *The Sunday Times* resigned after the hoax was revealed, and Kujau was sentenced to four years in prison.

DID YOU KNOW?

Konrad Kujau sold his fake diaries to media outlets via an intermediary, Gerd Heinemann. The German journalist believed Kujau's story that the journals had been rescued from a plane that crashed after leaving Berlin in 1945. But although Heinemann was not in on the fraud, he was found to have scammed Kujau on a magazine deal and was also sentenced to four years in jail.

THE BIG BONE BLUFF

When British lawyer and amateur archaeologist Charles Dawson announced that he had discovered the top of a human skull and an ape-like jawbone in a gravel pit near Piltdown, East Sussex, he set the scientific community abuzz.

Distinguished evolutionists agreed that the bone fragments must have come from the same creature: a 500,000-year-old missing link between apes and humans. "Piltdown Man" remained an important though controversial part of evolutionary understanding for decades, and three of the men involved in the research were knighted for their contributions to science.

In 1953, however, it was revealed that Piltdown Man was not what he seemed; the jawbone was ape-like because it actually belonged to a 10-year-old orangutan; the teeth had been filed down to simulate age; the human skull was medieval; the bones had been chemically aged. It was a complete hoax, and Charles Dawson remains the prime suspect.

RADIUM ALL THE RAGE

The radioactive element radium, discovered by Marie and Pierre Curie in 1898, was used as a cancer treatment in the early twentieth century. It soon became regarded as a cure-all treatment, and what you might call radium fever started to spread.

The dangerous element was put to use in various products, including toothpaste, medicines, cosmetics, energy tablets, hair treatments and even health drinks. Between the 1940s and 1970s, American children routinely had radioactive rods stuck up their noses to prevent problems with their hearing and tonsils – a treatment later found to increase the risk of brain cancer.

DID YOU KNOW?

From the 1920s to the 1970s, thousands of shoe shops in many countries used "pedoscopes" to X-ray customers' feet for shoe fittings. The machines were still in use in the 1970s, despite decades of reports of radiation damage, particularly to shop staff. In the 1950s, the British Home Office did take some action: they required pedoscopes to carry safety notices restricting users to just 12 fittings a year.

LONG LIVE THE QUEEN?

DATE: 2015

When the BBC broadcast journalist Ahmen Khawaja reported on Twitter that the Queen had died, the tweet was swiftly deleted, and Khawaja claimed that she had been victim of a prank after leaving her phone unattended.

In fact, she had confused a BBC rehearsal for the Queen's death with the real thing, and neglected to fact-check the momentous event before tweeting. Always an error for a journalist.

A NEW COCK-UP

The Coca-Cola Company reacted to the challenge posed by archrival Pepsi by shaking up its famous beverage. It unveiled bold new branding and a new sweeter recipe: the first for 99 years.

The gamble that became known as "New Coke" did not pay off. Fans of the original Coca-Cola did not take kindly to the change, and the company received thousands of phone calls in complaint. Groups such as the "Old Cola Drinkers of America" were set up to protest the decision.

Just three months later, the original recipe was back on the shelves as "Coca-Cola Classic". It was soon outselling its controversial younger sibling, which was later renamed Coke II and eventually quietly removed from sale.

DID YOU KNOW?

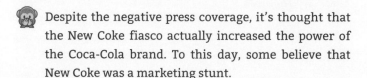

Despite the negative press coverage, it's thought that the New Coke fiasco actually increased the power of the Coca-Cola brand. To this day, some believe that New Coke was a marketing stunt.

Coca-Cola Company CEO Roberto Goizueta received many letters of complaint about New Coke, including one asking for the valuable autograph of "one of the dumbest executives in American business history".

When Coca-Cola fans heard their favourite drink was being changed, panic buying set in. One man in San Antonio, Texas, bought $1,000 of original-recipe Coke to hoard in his basement.

In 1985, the Old Cola Drinkers of America brought a lawsuit against the Coca-Cola Company on the grounds of false advertising in order to try to force them to bring back the original recipe. They lost in court, but were instrumental in bringing back old-school Coca-Cola through petitions and protests.

NO KEBAB JOKES PLEASE

DATE: 1846

When a group of 87 pioneers, led by Jacob and George Donner, travelled west from Illinois to make a new life for themselves in California, they didn't find the paradise they were hoping for.

The Donner party first travelled with a larger train of pioneers on an established route, but in Wyoming they broke off to take a newly discovered shortcut through the Sierra Nevada mountains. The route promised to save them 400 miles, but it was rough going and the group lost waggons and cattle in the rocky terrain.

At the end of October 1846, the party made it to their final mountain pass, but found their way blocked by deep snow. They were stranded and quickly ran out of food. First, they ate their cattle, then their horses, then their dogs; then they resorted to cannibalism. When rescue groups arrived in spring, less than half of the Donner party were left.

A KODAK MOMENT

DATE: 1975

Today, the American company Kodak, founded in 1892, is still known for old-fashioned camera film and printing. But the venerable business actually created one of the first digital cameras in 1975, way ahead of their competitors.

Instead of developing the idea, however, they failed to see its potential value. When Kodak executives were shown the digital camera, the response was that "no one would ever want to look at their pictures on a television set". The technology was buried until the 1990s, when it was utilized by Japanese companies such as Sony. Kodak caught up, but was soon undercut by cheaper competitors.

In 2009, Kodak stopped selling camera film, and in 2012 the company filed for bankruptcy.

 **DID YOU KNOW?**

Xerox, the company that introduced the photocopier, had a renowned research division in the 1970s that pioneered the personal computer, the graphical interface and more, but their executives were more interested in photocopy machines.

BLOCKBUSTED

DATE: 2000

Do you remember Blockbuster Video? The video rental giant was once worth $5 billion and had 9,000 stores around the world.

In 2000, the company was offered the chance to purchase a fledgling company that rented DVDs by post. The new company's owner, Reed Hastings, was asking for $50 million. Blockbuster's CEO dismissed the young firm as a "very small niche business", and declined the opportunity.

That "small niche business" was Netflix, which went on to pioneer on-demand video streaming and, as of March 2018, was worth more than $150 billion (more than Disney) and is largely responsible for companies like Blockbuster disappearing from the high street.

THE DARIEN DISASTER

Darien was an area in what is now Panama, where Scottish pioneers attempted to establish a colony to rival England's North American settlements.

The area was inhospitable swampland and already claimed by Spain, but the Scottish-led Darien Expedition nevertheless attracted a third of the nation's entire capital, with many Scots personally investing, and more than a thousand sailed on the first voyage to South America. Many settlers died en route, while disease, hunger and Spanish attacks killed hundreds more on arrival.

Darien was abandoned eight months later, but two more expeditions would meet a similar fate before the project was called off altogether. More than 2,000 Scots died. The scheme devastated the Scottish economy and is blamed for the country entering a union with England, reverberations of which are still being felt today.

MASSIVE MELTDOWN

DATE: APRIL 1986

In February 1986, Ukraine's energy minister stated that a meltdown at the nuclear power plant in Chernobyl could only occur in "one in 10,000 years". Unfortunately, that one year was 1986.

In April, engineers working on the cooling system made a mistake that resulted in a reactor overheating and exploding, blowing the roof off. Because the reactors at Chernobyl were not adequately contained, nuclear debris spilled out of the plant and deadly radiation was released high into the atmosphere.

The effects were noticed in Sweden before the Soviet Union admitted anything, and residents of Pripyat, one mile from the plant, were not evacuated for 36 hours. More than 350,000 people would eventually be displaced, and the contamination spread across Europe, with radioactive rain falling 1,500 miles away in Ireland. The nearby town of Chernobyl has been largely abandoned ever since.

DID YOU KNOW?

Five days after the disaster, a May Parade went ahead in Kiev, 70 miles from Chernobyl, to honour the workers at the plant, despite the radiation risk.

The Chernobyl explosion released 100 times more radiation than the nuclear bombs dropped on Japan at the end of World War Two.

It's estimated that the disaster will eventually cause between 10,000 and 50,000 deaths due to cancer.

The "Elephant's Foot" is a structure at the power plant still so radioactive that just five minutes of exposure to the still-deteriorating material would prove fatal.

An 800-foot concrete "sarcophagus" has been built to seal the Chernobyl reactor, after the old one, erected hurriedly after the disaster, started to collapse.

The 20-mile exclusion zone around the power station is today renowned as a thriving wildlife habitat.

THE LOST LAKE

DATE: 20 NOVEMBER 1980

Lake Peigneur was once a freshwater lake near the Gulf of Mexico in Louisiana, USA. It covered 1,300 acres, but was only about 10 feet deep, until one day in 1980 when the Texaco oil company started drilling.

Somebody got the calculations wrong, and the drill punctured a working salt mine under the lake. The lake disappeared into the mine, taking the drilling platform, 11 barges and 65 acres of land with it, including a car park. Incredibly, nobody died, even though the flooded mine had to be evacuated.

Water from the sea flowed backward through a canal and filled the empty void via a temporary 150-foot waterfall that turned Lake Peigneur into a 200-feet-deep saltwater lake.

ACCIDENTAL INCINERATION

DATE: MAY 2000

National Park Service officials started a large fire in the Bandelier National Monument park in New Mexico in May 2000 – but that wasn't the cock-up.

The blaze was a "prescribed fire", ironically intended to thin out a few hundred acres of dead vegetation that could pose a risk to local towns if a genuine wildfire started. The cock-up occurred when the "controlled burn" began to rage out of control, and fanned by high winds, the flames rampaged across 50,000 acres of forest.

By the time 1,000 fire fighters had brought the inferno under control, the fire had caused chaos in the town of Los Alamos, displacing 18,000 people and causing $1 billion in property damage.

 **DID YOU KNOW?**

In 2003, a deer hunter who had got lost in a forest near San Diego, California, lit two fires to attract rescuers. The flames sparked a wildfire that destroyed 300,000 acres of forest, more than 2,000 homes, and killed 15 people. The fire starter was prosecuted, but escaped a prison sentence.

BOUND TO FAIL

In what is now known as the Battle of Red Cliffs, the great northern Chinese warlord Cao Cao led a force of 200,000 men by land and water against the much smaller combined southern forces of Liu Bei and Sun Quan. But the giant army proved hard to mobilize, and Cao Cao retreated to the Red Cliffs on the Yangtze River.

Cao Cao then made the decision to chain his ships together, in an attempt either to reduce seasickness or to create a floating fortress. The plan literally backfired when his enemies feigned surrender and used the opportunity to release a fleet of fire ships that devastated Cao Cao's chained vessels, which were unable to evade the flames.

Cao Cao was forced to make another humiliating retreat and conceded defeat soon afterward.

THE ERRONEOUS EDSEL

DATE: 1957

Edsel was a new line of automobiles developed by Ford to compete with American market leader General Motors.

The brand was launched with a sophisticated $12 million campaign that promised a car unlike any other. Mysterious advertisements teased "The Edsel is on its way", and a television special was commissioned: *The Edsel Show*, starring Bing Crosby and Frank Sinatra.

Ford built expectations so high that when people actually saw the mid-priced car they were underwhelmed. They didn't like the look, which was likened to "an Oldsmobile sucking a lemon", and they didn't like the Edsel name which, coupled with the car's unreliability, became a joke: "**E**very **D**ay **S**omething **E**lse **L**eaks".

First-year sales were two-thirds lower than hoped, and production was halted after two years. The Edsel left Ford with a bill of $350 million, equivalent to $2 billion today.

TWITTERSTORM

DATE: 2011

American tech company Microsoft found itself in hot water online after using the Japanese tsunami as an opportunity to plug their new Bing Internet browser on Twitter.

Microsoft pledged $1 to the rescue effort for every retweet (up to $100,000), but despite the donation they were heavily criticized for exploiting a disaster in which more than 15,000 people died.

Several hours later the company apologized and donated the full $100,000.

TWIT-TER

The American shoe designer Kenneth Cole attempted to take advantage of the Arab Spring uprising in Egypt by tweeting, "Millions are in uproar in #Cairo. Rumor is they heard our new spring collection is now available online", with a link to his website.

After criticism he apologized, "... in hindsight my attempt at humor regarding a nation liberating themselves against oppression was poorly timed and absolutely inappropriate." Cole later clarified, however, that he wasn't sorry for the tweet, because it had the intended effect: "... Our stock went up that day, our e-commerce business was better, the business at every one of our stores improved, and I picked up 3,000 new followers on Twitter. So on what criteria is this a gaffe?"

In 2013, Cole sent another self-promoting tweet in the midst of a political storm about the Syrian civil war: "Boots on the ground or not, let's not forget about sandals, pumps and loafers."

BAD ROBOT

"Tay" is an artificial intelligence chat robot created by Microsoft. The tech company unleashed Tay on Twitter in order to talk to members of the public as part of an experiment into machine learning.

Unfortunately, online trolls discovered how to game Tay's learning skills, and within 24 hours the robotic Twitter account was parroting highly offensive racist messages to thousands of followers. Tay was swiftly retired from public speaking.

CAUGHT NAPPING

DATE: 1836

During the Texas Revolution, General Santa Anna of Mexico led a force of more than 1,000 men against a smaller Texan rebel force led by General Sam Houston near the San Jacinto River. Following early skirmishes, Santa Anna decided to rest his troops before attacking the rebels.

On 21 April 1836, he allowed his men to take a siesta, even though half were fresh reinforcements, and did not post sentries to watch the enemy. That afternoon, the Texans launched a surprise attack and routed the sleepy Mexicans, killing 600 and capturing 700 in less than 20 minutes, while losing only nine of their own number. General Santa Anna was captured the next day.

The United States went on to claim Texas, and today General Houston is remembered by having the largest city in the state named in his honour.

HYDROGEN HUBRIS

DATE: 1937

In March 1936, the world's largest zeppelin airship, the *Hindenburg*, was launched in Germany. More than 800 feet long, the *Hindenburg* was constructed of gelatine-treated cotton and filled with gas. Non-flammable helium was preferred, but due to American export restrictions on the gas, highly flammable hydrogen was used instead. It would be a memorable decision.

On 3 May 1937, the *Hindenburg* set off across the Atlantic Ocean from Germany to the United States with 97 passengers. The ship was late to its New Jersey destination because of thunderstorms, so the captain opted for a quick high landing using mooring lines. Seconds after the ropes were dropped, the *Hindenburg* exploded with a huge bang. The airship skin burned up in seconds and the flaming steel frame collapsed onto the passenger cabin as it hit the ground. Leaking hydrogen had been ignited by static electricity, possibly caused by the thundery weather. Thirty-five passengers died.

DEADLY DECISION

A criminal investigation was launched after a patient had the wrong organ removed at a hospital in Carmarthenshire, UK.

The man underwent an operation to remove his diseased right kidney, but surgeons mistakenly removed his healthy left organ, and then had to perform a second procedure to try to limit the damage.

The patient developed blood poisoning and he died a month later. A medical student observing the operation had warned the surgeons that they were operating on the wrong kidney, but she was ignored. The doctors were acquitted after going on trial for manslaughter.

BEWARE ENEMIES BEARING GIFTS

The Mongol Emperor Genghis Khan is today remembered as a ferocious warmonger, but sometimes he just wanted to trade peacefully. He had something of a reputation even then, though, so people didn't always believe him.

On trying to trade peacefully with the shah of the Khwarezmid Empire, which ruled Iran and parts of Central Asia in the thirteenth century, Khan incurred the distrust of the shah who decided to capture his trade envoys. Khan sent three ambassadors to negotiate their release, but the shah decapitated one of them and sent the two others back to Khan with the head.

This was the last straw for the Mongol warlord, who reverted to type: he invaded and destroyed the empire.

TWEETS THAT BOMBED

The food website Epicurious posted two insensitive tweets the day after the Boston Marathon bombings, promoting "whole-grain cranberry scones" in "honor of Boston" after leading with "Boston, our hearts are with you. Here's a bowl of breakfast energy we could all use to start today."

After a predictable reaction, they added, "Our food tweets this morning were, frankly, insensitive. Our deepest sincere apologies."

RONALDOH!

Pepsi was forced to apologize after their Swedish subsidiary posted images online of a voodoo doll resembling Portuguese football star Ronaldo. The doll was pictured impaled with pins, tied to train tracks and having its head crushed by a Pepsi can.

The images were meant to be a humorous nod to an upcoming football match between the two nations, but Portuguese fans did not see the funny side.

TIME OFF

For more than 130 years, the Greenwich meridian in London has divided the eastern and western hemispheres at zero degrees longitude, a system used by navigators the world over.

It is the basis of Greenwich Mean Time, going back to an era when sailors would keep a clock on the ships synchronized with the Greenwich clock. But in 2015, it was revealed that the line had been in the wrong place all along. Researchers discovered that the meridian, currently represented in the Royal Observatory in Greenwich by a line of steel, should actually be 334 feet to the east, running through a café in Greenwich Park.

The error was caused because the original calculations did not account for the natural bulge of planet Earth.

OIL SHOCK

Piper Alpha was an oil rig situated 120 miles from Aberdeen, Scotland, in the North Sea. The platform was Britain's largest single source of crude oil and natural gas.

In July 1988, one of the rig pumps failed. To prevent a costly shutdown, a second pump was started, but workers were unaware that earlier maintenance work had removed a safety valve. A leak of flammable natural gas caused a series of huge explosions that engulfed the platform in a fireball. Terrified workers leapt into the water – and they were the lucky ones. One-hundred-and-sixty-seven men lost their lives. The huge fire destroyed the 14,000-tonne rig in 90 minutes, and burned for three weeks.

The eventual insurance bill soared to more than £2 billion. The rig's operator was blamed for poor safety procedures. It paid £66 million in compensation to the victims' families, but no charges were ever brought.

DEEP WATER

The *Deepwater Horizon* oil rig, leased by the oil company BP, was situated 40 miles off the coast of Louisiana, USA. It was destroyed after a natural gas leak caused an explosion that killed 11 rig workers and engulfed the rig in an uncontrollable inferno that caused its collapse into the sea.

The sinking caused a rupture that leaked oil into the Gulf of Mexico for many weeks – four million barrels by the time it was plugged. It was the largest oil spill in the United States, causing widespread environmental damage. BP and associated companies Halliburton and Transocean were blamed for various engineering mistakes and a failure to prevent the explosion after the gas leak.

The disaster was one of the most expensive cock-ups in history, costing BP around $50 billion in total. Several individuals were charged with crimes, but none received prison sentences.

HUBBLE TROUBLE

The Hubble Space Telescope was launched in April 1990, after more than 20 years of painstaking development and $1.5 billion spent. When NASA received the first images back from the probe, however, they were blurry – not unusable, but definitely blurry. An investigation revealed that the 8-foot mirror Hubble used to capture images was the wrong shape.

In 1993, seven astronauts made a pioneering repair mission to the telescope and were able to rectify the optical error while in orbit 350 miles above the Earth's surface. Today, Hubble continues to send back superb images of deep space.

DID YOU KNOW?

In 2013, keen-eyed NASA followers spotted an image taken by a pair of $800 million rover vehicles on Mars which caused great hilarity online. While manoeuvring on the Red Planet, the rovers had left clear tracks in the dust that vaguely resembled a male sex organ. It was thought to be entirely accidental, and absolutely not a cock-up.

INDEPENDENCE NAY

DATE: 4 JULY 2014

The clothing company American Apparel posted an image on their Tumblr blog for Independence Day. The picture featured plumes of smoke in the sky, and was presumably intended as a patriotic image evoking Fourth of July fireworks.

Unfortunately, their chosen image was an edited version of an infamous photo capturing the immediate aftermath of the 1986 *Challenger* space shuttle disaster in which seven astronauts died. The company later claimed that the insensitive post was by a young employee who "was born after the tragedy and unaware of the event".

THE CHARGE OF THE LIGHT BRIGADE

During the Battle of Balaclava in the Crimean War, British Army officer Captain Nolan was dispatched with an order for the cavalry force (the Light Brigade) to prevent Russians from taking British heavy guns.

Lord Lucan, overall commander of the cavalry, could not see the guns at risk, and complained. Nolan, a proud man who did not like Lucan, replied that the cavalry should attack immediately: "There, my lord, is your enemy! There are your guns!" he said, waving vaguely toward the Russians.

Irritated and confused, Lucan ordered the Light Brigade – led by one Lord Cardigan – to charge against a different set of waiting Russian artillery batteries. Seven hundred cavalry officers rode into enemy guns on three sides, and in the ensuing carnage, 107 men were killed (including Nolan), 187 were wounded, 50 captured and 400 horses were lost.

Lord Cardigan, who survived the charge, was Lord Lucan's brother-in-law. When Lucan told him of the order, he knew that the Light Brigade would have no chance against the Russian guns. "There must be some mistake. I shall never be able to bring a single man back."

"I cannot help that," replied Lucan.

MAIL MIX-UP

DATE: DECEMBER 2016

An Australian man returned home from work to find that a demolition crew had levelled a house he had owned for 15 years.

Steve Ballas received a call from a friend who told him that his building was being demolished, but he thought he was joking. When he realized he wasn't, he rushed home, but was too late to save the three-bedroom house in a suburb of Sydney.

Ballas owned number 198, and the demolition team were contracted to destroy number 200. The wrecking crew reportedly failed to notice the incorrect house number because it was hidden by junk mail.

DON'T TRUST THE INTERNET

DATE: MARCH 2016

A demolition firm blamed a glitch in Google Maps for leading them to knock down the wrong house in Rowlett, Texas, USA.

The wrecking crew tore down the building at 7601 Calypso Drive instead of 7601 Cousteau Drive – a block away – because Google Maps had the two locations mixed up. The house had suffered damage during a tornado a couple of months earlier, and the owners were waiting on insurance money before they made any repairs. At least they wouldn't have had any trouble making a claim second time round.

A TWO-FOR-ONE JOB

A group of city contractors in Baltimore, USA, were hired to complete an emergency demolition of an old house that was in danger of falling down. It was all going well, until the digger they were using knocked a large pile of bricks onto the neighbouring property – a former pet shop called Laundry Mutt that was supposed to remain intact and had recently been bought for $160,000.

But when the smoke cleared it was evident that the first floor had been destroyed. The incident was caught on camera for posterity and soon went viral online, ensuring the wrecking crew's embarrassment for years to come.

 DID YOU KNOW?

> A scheduled demolition of a concrete silo in Denmark ended in disaster in April 2018 after the 53-metre-tall structure toppled in the wrong direction and damaged a cultural centre containing a library and music school.

> In 2015, a huge controlled demolition of the six remaining Red Road tower blocks in Glasgow, Scotland, once the tallest buildings in Europe, did not go entirely to plan and when the dust settled two of them were left with more floors than were bargained for. They were later taken down using a high-reach excavator.

MISSING: ONE PUB

A Staffordshire town once managed to lose a pub. The White Lion pub in Stafford, UK, was dismantled in the late 1970s to make way for a new road, with the proviso that the inn would be re-erected on a new site. The bricks, wood and interior fittings were put into storage, but then the pub seems to have been forgotten about.

In 2004, council workers admitted that nobody knew where the pub was because no records were kept, and the people involved had long since retired.

THE *VASA*

King Adolphus of Sweden was keen for his country to be the pre-eminent naval force in the Baltic, and in 1626 ordered the construction of the most impressive warship ever built in the country.

On Adolphus's orders the *Vasa* boasted 64 bronze cannons across two decks to beat his Polish rivals, making her the most powerful battleship of her day. But even during construction, his boatbuilders warned that she didn't carry enough ballast to balance her heavy guns. Adolphus ignored the naysayers.

In 1628, the *Vasa* was launched on her maiden voyage in Stockholm harbour in front of a huge crowd, who watched aghast as she heeled violently in gusts of wind. Water rushed into the gun decks, and she was unable to right herself. *Vasa* sank with the loss of 30 lives.

SURGICAL SLIP-UP

DATE: FEBRUARY 1995

When a Florida man was told his severely diseased leg had to be amputated, he probably didn't think the news could get much worse. But when he awoke from the operation, he still had his diseased leg, and the other leg had disappeared.

The surgeon in charge had been halfway through the amputation when a nurse told him that he was cutting through the wrong limb. At that point it was too late to undo the damage, and the amputation continued.

The surgeon was suspended from practising medicine, fined and reviled in the media. The patient received $1.2 million in damages, and his condemned leg was removed at another hospital.

 DID YOU KNOW?

> A 2007 study concluded that there could be up to 3,000 "wrong-site procedures" – where surgeons operate on the wrong part of the body – in the US every year.

> According to a US report, between 2005 and 2012, there were almost 800 incidents of surgeons leaving medical tools inside patients' bodies after operations, resulting in 16 deaths.

BEYOND-THE-GRAVE ERROR

When US tech giant Apple launched the iPhone 6, comedian Joan Rivers was one of the celebrities who promoted the new device on Facebook and Instagram. Nothing unusual there, apart from the fact that Rivers had been dead for two weeks. The social media postings were obviously scheduled before her death, and someone had forgotten to remove them.

DODGY DEFENCES

After the experience of World War One, France built a system of defences along its borders with Italy, Switzerland and, most importantly, Germany. The Maginot Line consisted of hundreds of sunken gun batteries, bunkers and anti-tank obstacles stretching for hundreds of miles and costing billions of francs.

The line was designed to delay an invasion force to allow time for a counter-attack. Crucially, the Maginot Line was weak along France's boundary with Belgium. France hoped that the Maginot defences would allow them to concentrate their defensive forces along the Belgian border.

In May 1940, Hitler made a mockery of this plan, invading France via the Netherlands and neutral Belgium. In some respects, the Maginot Line worked as planned, but the French defence failed to materialize and the country was overrun in six weeks.

 **DID YOU KNOW?**

The Ardennes forest, between France and Belgium, where the Maginot Line was weakest, was declared by French General Philippe Pétain as "impenetrable". When the Germans invaded in 1940, however, the forest did not cause them too many problems.

CLEARED FOR TAKE-OFF?

A mechanic was working on a plane in a hangar at Baton Rouge Airport, Louisiana, USA, when she started up an engine in order to clean it. Unfortunately, the throttle had been left at 85 per cent, and as the engine spooled up to almost full power, the 30-tonne passenger plane careered around the hangar and crashed into two other similar planes, causing serious damage.

The three planes were valued at $50 million, and the repair bill easily ran into seven figures.

CRUDE CONDIMENTS

DATE: 2015

When a German man used his mobile phone to scan the QR code on the back of a bottle of Heinz tomato ketchup, he was surprised to find himself directed to a pornography website.

The codes were introduced by Heinz as part of a design-your-own-label contest, but the ketchup giant let the website expire while the codes were still on bottles. An adult entertainment firm took advantage of that fact and snapped up the web domain for a saucy prank.

Daniel Korell, who spotted the error, informed Heinz, "Your ketchup is probably not for minors." The company apologized, and the pornography provider offered Korell a free subscription.

NOT-SO-FUNNY FALLOUT

Public relations executive Justine Sacco made a spectacular public relations gaffe after posting a "joke" on Twitter to her 170 followers about Africa and AIDS before getting on a flight to South Africa.

When she landed in Cape Town 11 hours later, her tweet had been seen by millions, and Twitter was ablaze with thousands of angry messages condemning what Sacco had thought was a throwaway message.

She lost her job amid a global media storm, and eventually spent time volunteering in Ethiopia.

CLOSE THAT DOOR

When the Ottoman Turks laid siege to the Byzantine capital Constantinople, the city's defences held up for more than 50 days, but they might have lasted longer if they hadn't kept leaving the doors open.

On 29 May 1453, a soldier returning from a raid forgot to shut a small gate in the city walls. The Turks spotted the opening and 50 of them surged through. Although soon killed, they managed to fly Ottoman flags on the city walls.

Meanwhile, the Byzantine Emperor Constantine XI unlocked a gate to allow a wounded commander to retreat. When his troops saw him leaving, they followed, encouraging a Turkish attack. When the struggling defenders saw the Ottoman flags they panicked, thinking the city was taken, and were slaughtered as they tried to escape.

NO-HIO?

DATE: 1953

Ohio joined the United States on
1 March 1803, but technically it did
not become a state until the 1950s.

During planning for the state's 150th anniversary,
somebody discovered that an official state
charter was never filed. Ohio Congressman
George Bender introduced a bill in Congress to
remedy the situation, and in 1953 President
Eisenhower signed legislation officially
confirming that Ohio existed.

WRONG TURN

One of the most famous deaths in history, the assassination of Archduke Franz Ferdinand of Austria in Sarajevo, sparked World War One. However, Ferdinand's death might not have occurred had his drivers known where they were going.

The archduke and his wife Sophie had already survived an earlier bombing attempt by Serbian nationalists that day, after the device exploded under another car in their motorcade. The royal couple decided not to flee the city but instead, unexpectedly, to visit the victims of the bombing in hospital; but they did not tell their drivers at the head of the motorcade, who followed the official route. When word of the intended destination got to the front car, the motorcade came to a halt.

By terrible chance, another assassin, Gavrilo Princip, was waiting for just such an opportunity. He spotted the archduke's stalled open-roof vehicle and was able to walk up and shoot both him and his wife.

FRIENDLY FIRE FAIL

DATE: 1788

During the Austro–Turkish War of 1787–91, confused Austrian soldiers started an Austro–Austro War with catastrophic consequences.

An army under the command of Emperor Joseph II marched to Karánsebes, in what is now Romania, to fight a force of Ottoman Turks. One evening, a group of Austrian cavalry hussars set up camp and got to work on a barrel of peach schnapps. When Austrian infantry arrived, the drunken hussars took them for Turks and fired at them. Austrian commanders confused the skirmish for a Turkish assault, and ordered the artillery to fire on their own troops. When the Turks eventually did arrive, they found 10,000 dead or wounded Austrians.

PRIZE DUMMIES

DATE: 2014

The Indian branch of advertising giant Ogilvy & Mather apologized after creating an advert for a mattress firm that featured Malala Yousafzai, renowned for her journey from being shot by the Taliban aged 14 to becoming a global education campaigner.

The cartoon ads graphically depicted the Nobel Peace Prize winner being shot, then literally "bouncing back" to success from one of the company's mattresses!

TRUST NO ONE

When the Spanish explorer Hernán Cortés landed in what is now Mexico, the Americas had only been discovered 30 years before, and the giant Aztec Empire ruled the indigenous people.

Although the Aztecs were dominant in their own land, they were ignorant of Europeans and their intentions, and they made a gigantic error in not seeing them as a threat. But Cortés had only brought a few hundred men with him, and there were millions of Aztecs. Cortés asked to see the leader, Montezuma II, and he and his soldiers were duly taken to the capital of the empire, Tenochtitlan, where they slaughtered the emperor's bodyguards and took him hostage.

From there, Cortés was eventually able to direct a Spanish takeover of the entire empire, and within decades, the natives were largely wiped out.

TRUST NO ONE AND LEARN FROM HISTORY

DATE: 1532

Thirteen years later, another Spanish explorer, Francisco Pizarro, pulled an almost identical trick on the Inca Empire in South America.

Incredibly, news of the Aztecs' fate had not reached the all-powerful Inca, which meant Pizarro was able to dupe the Inca leader Atahualpa into a meeting. The Spaniard had fewer than 200 men with him, so again he wasn't seen as a threat – so much so that Atahualpa got very drunk before the meeting. But with superior firepower and horses – which the Inca had never seen before – the small band of Spaniards easily overpowered Atahualpa's bodyguard of 5,000 men and took the leader captive.

Atahualpa was eventually executed, and Pizarro emulated Cortés by taking over the Inca Empire with the help of the indigenous people who were also ignorant of his intentions.

 **DID YOU KNOW?**

When the Spaniards arrived in the Aztec Empire, the natives followed them around with burning incense. The Spanish thought it was a mark of respect, but in actual fact the Aztecs thought the Spanish sailors stank and they were masking the smell.

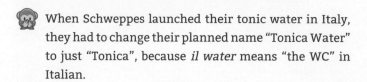

DID YOU KNOW?

When Schweppes launched their tonic water in Italy, they had to change their planned name "Tonica Water" to just "Tonica", because *il water* means "the WC" in Italian.

In 2015, McDonald's ran an ad campaign that highlighted how they changed their company billboards in response to tragic events such as 9/11 and the Boston Marathon bombing. It didn't have the expected impact; many accused the company of taking advantage of tragedies.

A company from Uttar Pradesh, India, attracted global condemnation in 2015 after launching a line of ice-cream cones named "Hitler", complete with branding emblazoned with an image of the Nazi dictator.

Parker Pen launched a promotional campaign for its pen ink in Spain with the tagline "Avoid embarrassment – use Parker SuperQuink". Unfortunately, once translated, it meant that the company's quick-drying ink would help users "avoid pregnancy".

If you're interested in finding out more about our books, find us on Facebook at **Summersdale Publishers** and follow us on Twitter at **@Summersdale**.

www.summersdale.com